debbie macomber

Popular author Debbie Macomber has discovered that women's fiction and knitting go together like a hand and glove — a knit glove, of course.

In her books *The Shop on Blossom Street* and *A Good Yarn*, Debbie introduces us to two groups of women from highly diverse backgrounds. The women join knitting classes at a small yarn shop in Seattle and soon discover that friendship truly knows no boundaries.

With more than 60 million copies of her books in print and an ever-growing base of fans who eagerly await the release of each new novel, you might think that Debbie is simply too busy to do anything but write. However, Debbie is herself an avid knitter who believes strongly in "giving back" to her community. One way she accomplishes this is by drawing attention to worthy causes through her books.

It was while working on *The Shop on Blossom Street* that Debbie learned about an organization called Warm Up America! Knitters and crocheters create 7" x 9" blocks for this charity group. The blocks are joined into blankets and donated to the needy. Debbie became one of the first board members for Warm Up America!, and she continues to work tirelessly on its behalf.

In fact, Debbie is delighted to let you know that all her profits from the sales of both *Knit Along with Debbie Macomber* pattern books — *The Shop on Blossom Street* and *A Good Yarn* — will be donated to Warm Up America! to support their work in communities across the United States. She urges everyone who uses these patterns to take a few minutes to knit or crochet a block for this worthy cause. On page 38, you will find out how, with just a little bit of yarn, you can make a real difference.

Debbie also hopes that **this collection of eleven knit baby blankets**, beginning with the beautiful Baby Blocks pattern by Ann Norling, will inspire you to discover the rich rewards of knitting for yourself and those you love.

LEISURE ARTS, INC.
Little Rock, Arkansas

a word from
LEISURE ARTS
and MIRA books

Read The Books That Inspired the Projects

Debbie Macomber's fan-favorite novel, *The Shop on Blossom Street*, introduced us to four fascinating women who share their joys and heartaches while learning to knit in a Seattle yarn shop. This best-selling story is now joined by Debbie's next book in the fiction series: *A Good Yarn* — and what a good yarn it is! Three women of varying ages learn the art of knitting in this delightful tale of love and unexpected friendship.

And now you can experience the rewards of knitting, just like the women of Blossom Street! Leisure Arts is pleased to offer two knitting instruction books as companions to the novels.

Knit Along with Debbie Macomber — The Shop on Blossom Street has complete instructions for 11 darling baby blankets. Also included are patterns for three sample blocks that you can make to contribute to Debbie's favorite nonprofit organization, Warm Up America!

The second knitting book, *Knit Along with Debbie Macomber— A Good Yarn*, contains 12 patterns for beautiful hats, socks, sweaters, a poncho, and more.

Laced with excerpts from the novels, each knitting instruction book retains the warm, friendly atmosphere created by this gifted author. Read Debbie Macomber's insightful stories of love, then knit up a little creativity from Leisure Arts.

knit along with
DEBBIE MACOMBER

LOOK FOR THESE HEARTWARMING STORIES ABOUT KNITTING AND FRIENDSHIP AT BOOKSTORES EVERYWHERE.

Leaflet #4132

Leaflet #4135

Wonderful knitting leaflets inspired by the novels *The Shop on Blossom Street* and *A Good Yarn*

To find out more about Debbie Macomber, visit www.debbiemacomber.com or www.mirabooks.com

For information about these and other Leisure Arts leaflets, call **1.800.526.5111** or visit **www.leisurearts.com**

LEISURE ARTS
the art of everyday living

2

meet the women

from *The Shop on Blossom Street*

LYDIA HOFFMAN

The first time I saw the empty store on Blossom Street I thought of my father. It reminded me so much of the bicycle shop he had when I was a kid. Even the large display windows, shaded by a colorful striped awning, were the same. A week after viewing the property, I signed my name, Lydia Hoffman, to the two-year lease. I opened A Good Yarn on the last Tuesday in April. Most of the yarn had arrived on Friday and I'd spent the weekend sorting it by weight and color. I'd bought a secondhand cash register, refinished the counter and set up racks of knitting supplies. I was ready for business.

I learned to knit while undergoing chemotherapy. Over the years I've become an accomplished knitter. Dad always joked that I had enough yarn to open my own store; recently I decided he was right.

Now I have my own shop and I think the best way to get customers in the door is to offer knitting classes … I've chosen a simple baby blanket to start with. The pattern's by one of my favorite designers, Ann Norling, and uses the basic knit and purl stitches.

This shop was my affirmation of life. I was willing to invest everything I had to make it a success. Like the Viking conqueror who came ashore and burned his ships behind him, I had set my course. Succeed or go under.

3

The angry exchange of words with her married son had distressed Jacqueline Donovan. She'd honestly tried to keep her negative feelings regarding her daughter-in-law to herself. But when Paul phoned to tell her Tammie Lee was five and a half months pregnant, Jacqueline had lost her temper and said things she shouldn't have.

For the life of her, Jacqueline couldn't understand why her sensible son would marry this little girl from the swamps, when so many of her friends' daughters were interested in him. Paul called Tammie Lee his southern belle, but all Jacqueline saw was a hillbilly.

Reese, Jacqueline's husband, studied her as if he was really noticing her for the first time. "Why are you so angry?"

"Because I'm afraid of losing my son." Paul and her close relationship with him was the only consolation she had in a life that brought her little joy. Now she'd done something stupid and insulted her son.

"Call him back and apologize."

Jacqueline nodded. "I plan to do something else, too. I saw a sign in the window of that new knitting shop. I'm going to register for a knitting class. The sign says the beginning project is a baby blanket. I might not like Tammie Lee, but I will be the best grandmother I can."

Carol strolled along her usual route. Then on a whim she headed east ... until she came to Blossom Street. A number of buildings were being renovated, with freshly painted storefronts and a green-and-white awning over the florist's shop.

Next to the florist was a yarn store. A woman sat in a rocking chair inside, her hands busy with a pair of needles. A large ball of lime-green yarn rested on her lap.

Because she had nothing better to do, Carol walked through the door. She wasn't sure what drew her into the shop.

The petite woman greeted her with a shy smile. "Hello and welcome to A Good Yarn. Do you knit?"

The question was inevitable. "No, but I'd like to learn someday."

"Then you've come to the right place. I have a beginners' class starting next Friday. I thought I'd have everyone work on a baby blanket."

Carol froze and tears sprang instantly to her eyes. "Perhaps I will sign up for the class," she said, fingering a ball of bright yellow yarn.

These days, Carol looked everywhere for signs and portents, and she had frequent conversations with God. Without a doubt she knew she'd been sent to this shop. It was His way of letting her know He was about to answer her prayers. When she went in for the fertilization process this third and final time, she would be successful. In the not-too-distant future she was going to need a baby blanket for her child.

Alix Townsend smashed her cigarette butt into the cracked concrete sidewalk with the toe of her knee-high black combat boots. The manager of Blossom Street Video frowned on employees smoking in the break room and rather than put up with his snide comments, she chose to smoke outside. He was right about one thing, though. All this construction was killing business.

She burrowed her hands into her black leather jacket and glared down the street at the dust and debris. Then she concentrated on the other side of the street. All the storefronts were newly painted. The new florist shop had already opened, as well as a beauty parlor. The shop situated between them remained something of a mystery. A Good Yarn. Either it was a bookstore or a knitting shop. In this neighborhood neither would last long, she suspected.

Alix crossed the street. She peered through the window and saw a handmade sign offering knitting classes. If she started knitting, it would get the court off her back. Maybe she could do something about those community-service hours Judge Roper had thrown at her.

"Hi," Alex said, letting her voice boom when she walked in the door. "I want to know about that knitting class." Her case worker had once suggested knitting as a means of anger management. Maybe it would work.

baby blocks

Designer Ann Norling's simple pattern is Lydia's choice for her first beginning knitters' class. Lydia says the basic knit and purl stitches make the Baby Blocks pattern challenging enough to keep you interested, but not so difficult as to discourage you.

◖■▢▢ EASY

Lydia's Tip: A row counter may be handy to keep track of which pattern row you're on.

Finished Size: 34" x 45" (86.5 cm x 114.5 cm)

MATERIALS

Medium/Worsted Weight Yarn:
[3.5 ounces, 166 yards, 100 grams, 152 meters per skein]: 8 skeins
29" (73.5 cm) or 36" (91.5 cm) Circular knitting needle, size 8 (5 mm) **or** size needed for gauge
Yarn needle

GAUGE: In pattern,
20 sts = 4" (10 cm)

Gauge Swatch: 4¼" (10.75 cm) wide
Cast on 21 sts.
Work same as Bottom Border.
Bind off all sts in pattern.

BOTTOM BORDER
Cast on 171 sts.

Row 1: K3, (P3, K3) across.

Row 2: P3, (K3, P3) across.

Row 3: K3, (P3, K3) across.

Rows 4 and 5: P3, (K3, P3) across.

Row 6: K3, (P3, K3) across.

Row 7: P3, (K3, P3) across.

Rows 8 and 9: K3, (P3, K3) across.

Row 10: P3, (K3, P3) across.

Row 11: K3, (P3, K3) across.

Row 12: P3, (K3, P3) across.

Instructions continued on page 11.

Although I'd taught knitting for a number of years, I'd never worked with such an eclectic group as the women in my small beginners' class. They had absolutely nothing in common. The three of them sat stiffly at the table in the back of the store, not exchanging a word.

— Lydia

carol's sunshine

Traditional yellow baby blankets are irresistible to Carol, who has always wanted to be a mother. This cable-patterned wrap uses cotton yarn in her favorite hue, but would be just as delightful in any color you choose.

◼◼◼◻ **INTERMEDIATE**

Lydia's Tip: Lace is combined with cables, working Garter Stitch between them instead of the usual Reverse Stockinette Stitch.

Finished Size: 34" x 42" (86.5 cm x 106.5 cm)

MATERIALS

100% Cotton Medium/Worsted Weight Yarn
[4 ounces, 200 yards, 113 grams, 182 meters per skein]: 6 skeins
29" (73.5 cm) or 36" (91.5 cm) Circular knitting needle, size 10 (6 mm) **or** size needed for gauge
Cable needle
Yarn needle

GAUGE: In Stockinette Stitch,
16 sts and 20 rows = 4" (10 cm)

STITCH GUIDE

CABLE (uses 4 sts)
Slip next 2 sts onto cable needle and hold in **back** of work, K2 from left needle, K2 from cable needle.

BLANKET

Cast on 135 sts.

Rows 1-9: Purl across.

When instructed to slip a stitch that will be used in a decrease, always slip as if to **knit**.

Row 10 (Right side)**:** P4, [slip 1, K1, PSSO *(Figs. 5a & b, page 44)*], YO *(Fig. 1a, page 43)*, K3, YO, K2 tog *(Fig. 3, page 44)*, ★ P2, K4, P2, slip 1, K1, PSSO, YO, K3, YO, K2 tog; repeat from ★ across to last 4 sts, P4.

Row 11 AND ALL WRONG SIDE ROWS: Purl across.

Row 12: P4, K2, YO, [slip 1, K2 tog, PSSO *(Fig. 7, page 45)*], YO, K2, ★ P2, work Cable, P2, K2, YO, slip 1, K2 tog, PSSO, YO, K2; repeat from ★ across to last 4 sts, P4.

Instructions continued on page 10.

Carol's my star pupil, already half done with the baby blanket, and eyeing other projects. She's been coming by the shop at least twice a week, often staying to chat.

— *Lydia*

Row 14: P4, slip 1, K1, PSSO, YO, K3, YO, K2 tog, ★ P2, K4, P2, slip 1, K1, PSSO, YO, K3, YO, K2 tog; repeat from ★ across to last 4 sts, P4.

Row 16: P4, K2, YO, slip 1, K2 tog, PSSO, YO, K2, ★ P2, K4, P2, K2, YO, slip 1, K2 tog, PSSO, YO, K2; repeat from ★ across to last 4 sts, P4.

Row 18: P4, slip 1, K1, PSSO, YO, K3, YO, K2 tog, ★ P2, work Cable, P2, slip 1, K1, PSSO, YO, K3, YO, K2 tog; repeat from ★ across to last 4 sts, P4.

Row 20: P4, K2, YO, slip 1, K2 tog, PSSO, YO, K2, ★ P2, K4, P2, K2, YO, slip 1, K2 tog, PSSO, YO, K2; repeat from ★ across to last 4 sts, P4.

Row 22: P4, slip 1, K1, PSSO, YO, K3, YO, K2 tog, ★ P2, K4, P2, slip 1, K1, PSSO, YO, K3, YO, K2 tog; repeat from ★ across to last 4 sts, P4.

Repeat Rows 11-22 for pattern until Blanket measures approximately 41" (104 cm) from cast on edge, ending by working **Row 20**.

Last 8 Rows: Purl across.

Bind off all sts in **purl**.

Weave in all yarn ends.

Design by Rachel J. Terrill.

Baby Blocks continued from page 6.

BODY

Row 1: P3, K3, P3, K9, (P9, K9) across to last 9 sts, P3, K3, P3.

Row 2: K3, P3, K3, P9, (K9, P9) across to last 9 sts, K3, P3, K3.

Rows 3 and 4: Repeat Rows 1 and 2.

Row 5: K3, P3, K 12, P9, (K9, P9) across to last 18 sts, K 12, P3, K3.

Row 6: P3, K3, P 12, K9, (P9, K9) across to last 18 sts, P 12, K3, P3.

Rows 7 and 8: Repeat Rows 5 and 6.

Rows 9-11: Repeat Rows 1 and 2 once, then repeat Row 1 once **more**.

Rows 12 and 13: Repeat Row 2.

Rows 14-16: Repeat Rows 1 and 2 once, then repeat Row 1 once **more**.

Row 17: Repeat Row 6.

Rows 18-20: Repeat Rows 5 and 6 once, then repeat Row 5 once **more**.

Row 21: Repeat Row 2.

Rows 22-24: Repeat Rows 1 and 2 once, then repeat Row 1 once **more**.

Repeat Rows 1-24 for pattern until Blanket measures approximately 42" (106.5 cm) from cast on edge, ending by working **Row 12**.

TOP BORDER

Repeat Rows 1-12 of Bottom Border.

Bind off all sts in pattern.

Weave in all yarn ends.

Design by Ann Norling.

sleepy in seattle

Everyone at the yarn shop agrees that this is one of the softest baby blankets they've ever seen. It's made with a thick bouclé yarn in an all-over lace pattern. Jacqueline has promised to pass this pattern on to Alix just as soon as she's finished with it.

■■□□ EASY

Lydia's Tip: When working a basic lace pattern you'll find that for every YO there is a decrease and the original stitch count is maintained throughout. In this pattern, a garter ridge is formed between every two lace rows.

Finished Size: 32" x 42" (81.5 cm x 106.5 cm)

MATERIALS

Bulky Weight Yarn:
[4 ounces, 204 yards, 113 grams, 185 meters per skein]: 4 skeins
29" (73.5 cm) or 36" (91.5 cm) Circular knitting needle, size 10 (6 mm) **or** size needed for gauge
Yarn needle

GAUGE: In pattern, 12 sts = 4¼" (10.75 cm)

Gauge Swatch: 5"w x 4"h
(12.75 cm x 10 cm)
Cast on 14 sts.
Rows 1-3: Purl across.
Row 4 (Right side): P1, (YO, K2 tog) across to last st *(Figs. 1a-c, page 43 and Fig. 3, page 44)*, P1.
Row 5: Purl across.
Row 6: P1, (K2 tog, YO) across to last st, P1.
Rows 7-21: Repeat Rows 1-6 twice, then repeat Rows 1-3 once **more**.
Bind off all sts.

BLANKET
Cast on 90 sts.

Rows 1-6: Purl across.

Row 7 (Right side): P4, (YO, K2 tog) across to last 4 sts *(Figs. 1a-c, page 43 and Fig. 3, page 44)*, P4.

Row 8: Purl across.

Row 9: P4, (K2 tog, YO) across to last 4 sts, P4.

Rows 10-12: Purl across.

Row 13: P4, (YO, K2 tog) across to last 4 sts, P4.

Repeat Rows 8-13 for pattern until Blanket measures approximately 41" (104 cm) from cast on edge, ending by working Row 9.

Last 6 Rows: Purl across.

Bind off all sts in **purl**.

Weave in all yarn ends.

Design by Jean Lampe.

I'd had a bit of a challenge talking Jacqueline into staying in the class. There'd been a couple of rough moments when Alix dropped a stitch and let loose with a blue streak that nearly put Jacqueline in a coma. Immediately I suggested Alix find an alternative method of expressing her frustration. To my surprise, she apologized. Alix isn't so bad once you get to know her.

— Lydia

only the finest for amelia

Due to time constraints, Jacqueline was compelled to purchase a designer layette for her grandbaby's christening. However, she was determined to personalize the outfit. She knitted this dainty lace-panel wrap and its sewn-on border, and was often heard saying, "I should have learned to knit sooner!"

■■■■□ INTERMEDIATE

Lydia's Tip: The Border is worked separately across the width and sewn to the Center. When working three stitches all in one stitch, work into the front loop, moving the working yarn from back to front as necessary.

Finished Size: 34" x 40" (86.5 cm x 101.5 cm)

MATERIALS

Light Weight Yarn:
[5 ounces, 350 yards, 142 grams, 320 meters per skein]: 4 skeins
29" (73.5 cm) or 36" (91.5 cm) Circular knitting needle **and** Straight knitting needles for Borders, size 8 (5.00 mm) **or** size needed for gauge
Markers
¼" (7 mm) wide Ribbon - 5 yards
Tapestry needle

GAUGE: In Stockinette Stitch,
18 sts and 28 rows = 4" (10 cm)

CENTER

Cast on 123 sts.

Rows 1-21: Knit across.

Row 22 (Right side)**:** K 11, ★ place marker *(see Markers, page 41)*, SSK *(Figs. 4a-c, page 44)*, YO *(Figs. 1a-c, page 43)*, K2, K2 tog *(Fig. 3, page 44)*, YO, K1, YO, [slip 1 as if to **knit**, K2 tog, PSSO *(Fig. 7, page 45)*], YO, K1, YO, SSK, K2, YO, K2 tog, place marker, K 11; repeat from ★ across.

Row 23 AND ALL WRONG SIDE ROWS: (Knit to marker, purl to marker) 4 times, knit across.

Row 24: ★ Knit to marker, SSK, K3, YO, K2 tog, YO, K3, YO, SSK, YO, K3, K2 tog; repeat from ★ across to last marker, knit across.

Row 26: ★ Knit to marker, SSK, (K2, YO) twice, K2 tog, K1, SSK, (YO, K2) twice, K2 tog; repeat from ★ across to last marker, knit across.

Row 28: ★ Knit to marker, SSK, K1, YO, K3, YO, K2 tog, K1, SSK, YO, K3, YO, K1, K2 tog; repeat from ★ across to last marker, knit across.

Repeat Rows 22-29 until Center measures approximately 35" (89 cm) from cast on edge, ending by working **Row 22.**

Next 21 Rows: Knit across.

Bind off all sts.

Instructions continued on page 19.

Jacqueline came into the shop, bracelets jangling. She wore a tailored pantsuit that Carol considered far too formal for the occasion and carried not only her Gucci purse but a leather tote in which she kept her knitting. It was as if she expected everyone to notice she'd arrived and react accordingly. Actually, Carol didn't mind. She'd grown to like all the women in her knitting group.

lydia's baby cables

A modified cable runs through this sweet little blanket. It's one of Lydia's favorite patterns for baby shower gifts. Sometimes she makes a second blanket in a different color, then wraps them both in coordinating tissue paper for a lucky mom-to-be!

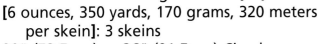 INTERMEDIATE

Lydia's Tip: The baby cables have a modified cable look that is formed without the use of a cable needle. A decrease is made without an immediate yarn over to compensate for the lost stitch, so the stitch count changes often. The right twist is used in the lacy diamond pattern to connect the top of each diamond to the next one.

Finished Size: 31" x 42" (78.5 cm x 106.5 cm)

MATERIALS

Medium/Worsted Weight Yarn: **MEDIUM 4**
[6 ounces, 350 yards, 170 grams, 320 meters per skein]: 3 skeins
29" (73.5 cm) or 36" (91.5 cm) Circular knitting needle, size 10 (6 mm) **or** size needed for gauge
Yarn needle

GAUGE: In Stockinette Stitch,
16 sts and 20 rows = 4" (10 cm)

STITCH GUIDE

RIGHT TWIST *(abbreviated RT)* (uses 2 sts)
K2 tog but do **not** slip sts off needle, knit first st again, slipping both sts off left needle.

BLANKET

Cast on 135 sts.

Rows 1-7: K1, (P1, K1) across.

Row 8 (Increase row)**:** (K1, P1) twice, increase by knitting in front and in back of next st *(Figs. 2a & b, page 44)*, (P1, K1) across: 136 sts.

Row 9: (K1, P1) twice, K3, P3, ★ K2, P 10, K2, P3; repeat from ★ across to last 7 sts, K3, (P1, K1) twice.

When instructed to slip a stitch that will be used in a decrease, always slip as if to **knit**.

Row 10 (Right side)**:** K1, (P1, K1) twice, P2, [slip 1, K2, PSSO *(Fig. 6, page 45)*], P2, ★ K2, K2 tog *(Fig. 3, page 44)*, YO *(Fig. 1a, page 43)*, RT, YO, SSK *(Figs. 4a-c, page 44)*, K2, P2, slip 1, K2, PSSO, P2; repeat from ★ across to last 5 sts, K1, (P1, K1) twice: 128 sts.

Row 11: (K1, P1) twice, K3, P2, ★ K2, P 10, K2, P2; repeat from ★ across to last 7 sts, K3, (P1, K1) twice.

Instructions continued on page 18.

16

I love to knit. There's a comfort to it that I can't entirely explain. The repetition of weaving the yarn around a needle and then forming a stitch creates a sense of purpose, of achievement, of progress.

—Lydia

Row 12: K1, (P1, K1) twice, P2, K1, YO, K1, P2, ★ K1, K2 tog, YO, K4, YO, SSK, K1, P2, K1, YO, K1, P2; repeat from ★ across to last 5 sts, K1, (P1, K1) twice: 136 sts.

Row 13: (K1, P1) twice, K3, P3, ★ K2, P 10, K2, P3; repeat from ★ across to last 7 sts, K3, (P1, K1) twice.

Row 14: K1, (P1, K1) twice, P2, slip 1, K2, PSSO, P2, ★ K2 tog, YO, K1, K2 tog, YO twice, SSK, K1, YO, SSK, P2, slip 1, K2, PSSO, P2; repeat from ★ across to last 5 sts, K1, (P1, K1) twice: 128 sts.

Row 15: (K1, P1) twice, K3, P2, ★ K2, P4, K1, P5, K2, P2; repeat from ★ across to last 7 sts, K3, (P1, K1) twice.

Row 16: K1, (P1, K1) twice, P2, K1, YO, K1, P2, ★ K2, YO, SSK, K2, K2 tog, YO, K2, P2, K1, YO, K1, P2; repeat from ★ across to last 5 sts, K1, (P1, K1) twice: 136 sts.

Row 17: (K1, P1) twice, K3, P3, ★ K2, P 10, K2, P3; repeat from ★ across to last 7 sts, K3, (P1, K1) twice.

Row 18: K1, (P1, K1) twice, P2, slip 1, K2, PSSO, P2, ★ K3, YO, SSK, K2 tog, YO, K3, P2, slip 1, K2, PSSO, P2; repeat from ★ across to last 5 sts, K1, (P1, K1) twice: 128 sts.

Row 19: (K1, P1) twice, K3, P2, ★ K2, P 10, K2, P2; repeat from ★ across to last 7 sts, K3, (P1, K1) twice.

Row 20: K1, (P1, K1) twice, P2, K1, YO, K1, P2, ★ K2, K2 tog, YO, RT, YO, SSK, K2, P2, K1, YO, K1, P2; repeat from ★ across to last 5 sts, K1, (P1, K1) twice: 136 sts.

Row 21: (K1, P1) twice, K3, P3, ★ K2, P 10, K2, P3; repeat from ★ across to last 7 sts, K3, (P1, K1) twice.

Row 22: K1, (P1, K1) twice, P2, slip 1, K2, PSSO, P2, ★ K1, K2 tog, YO, K4, YO, SSK, K1, P2, slip 1, K2, PSSO, P2; repeat from ★ across to last 5 sts, K1, (P1, K1) twice: 128 sts.

Row 23: (K1, P1) twice, K3, P2, ★ K2, P 10, K2, P2; repeat from ★ across to last 7 sts, K3, (P1, K1) twice.

Row 24: K1, (P1, K1) twice, P2, K1, YO, K1, P2, ★ K2 tog, YO, K1, K2 tog, YO twice, SSK, K1, YO, SSK, P2, K1, YO, K1, P2; repeat from ★ across to last 5 sts, K1, (P1, K1) twice: 136 sts.

Row 25: (K1, P1) twice, K3, P3, ★ K2, P4, K1, P5, K2, P3; repeat from ★ across to last 7 sts, K3, (P1, K1) twice.

Row 26: K1, (P1, K1) twice, P2, slip 1, K2, PSSO, P2, ★ K2, YO, SSK, K2, K2 tog, YO, K2, P2, slip 1, K2, PSSO, P2; repeat from ★ across to last 5 sts, K1, (P1, K1) twice: 128 sts.

Row 27: (K1, P1) twice, K3, P2, ★ K2, P 10, K2, P2; repeat from ★ across to last 7 sts, K3, (P1, K1) twice.

Row 28: K1, (P1, K1) twice, P2, K1, YO, K1, P2, ★ K3, YO, SSK, K2 tog, YO, K3, P2, K1, YO, K1, P2; repeat from ★ across to last 5 sts, K1, (P1, K1) twice: 136 sts.

Row 29: (K1, P1) twice, K3, P3, ★ K2, P 10, K2, P3; repeat from ★ across to last 7 sts, K3, (P1, K1) twice.

Repeat Rows 10-29 for pattern until Afghan measures approximately 41" (104 cm) from cast on edge, ending by working **Row 21**.

Next Row (Decrease row)**:** (K1, P1) twice, K2 tog, (P1, K1) across: 135 sts.

Last 6 Rows: K1, (P1, K1) across.

Bind off all sts in pattern.

Weave in all yarn ends.

Design by Rachel J. Terrill.

Only the Finest for Amelia continued from page 14.

BORDER
Cast on 11 sts **loosely**.

Row 1: Slip 1 as if to **purl**, K1, ★ YO, P2 tog *(Fig. 8, page 45)*, (K, P, K) **all** in next st; repeat from ★ across: 17 sts.

Row 2 (Right side)**:** (K3, YO, P2 tog) 3 times, K2.

Note: Loop a short piece of yarn around any stitch to mark Row 2 as **right** side.

Row 3: Slip 1 as if to **purl**, K1, (YO, P2 tog, K3) across.

Row 4: K2, ★ slip second st on right needle over first st, K1, slip second st on right needle over first st, YO, P2 tog, K2; repeat from ★ across: 11 sts.

Repeat Rows 1-4 until Border is long enough to fit completely around Center, allowing for ease at corners and ending by working **Row 4**.

Bind off all sts **loosely**.

FINISHING
Whipstitch straight edge of Border to Center *(Fig. 10, page 46)*, easing to fit at corners; whipstitch ends together.

Weave in all yarn ends.

Using photo as a guide for placement and beginning at bottom left corner, weave ribbon through inside eyelets of Border and tie in a bow.

Design by C. Strohmeyer.

boats for cameron

Three of the knitting class ladies worked together to create this nautical blanket as a surprise for a much-loved boy. The panels are worked individually, making this a good "shared" project.

◖■■■□ **INTERMEDIATE**

Lydia's Tip: Cables can be fun to make, because all it takes is a neat little trick to form a fabric that almost looks braided. Since the Panel is only twelve stitches wide, you can practice making the cables and see fast results.

Finished Size: 36" x 44" (91.5 cm x 112 cm)

MATERIALS

Bulky Weight Yarn:
[4 ounces, 155 yards, 113 grams, 140 meters per skein]:
    Blue - 5 skeins
    White - 2 skeins
Straight knitting needles **and** 29" (73.5 cm)
    Circular knitting needle for Borders,
    size 11 (8 mm) **or** size needed for gauge
Cable needle
Stitch holders - 5
Yarn needle

GAUGE: In Stockinette Stitch,
        12 sts and 16 rows = 4" (10 cm)

CABLE PANEL (Make 2)

With White and straight needles, cast on 12 sts.

Row 1: P1, K2, P6, K2, P1.

Row 2 (Right side)**:** K1, P2, K6, P2, K1.

Row 3: P1, K2, P6, K2, P1.

Row 4: K1, P2, slip next 3 sts onto cable needle and hold in **back** of work, K3 from left needle, K3 from cable needle, P2, K1.

Rows 5-11: Repeat Rows 1 and 2, 3 times; then repeat Row 1 once **more**.

Rows 12-151: Repeat Rows 4-11, 17 times; then repeat Rows 4-7 once **more**.

Slip stitches onto stitch holder.

Instructions continued on page 22.

BOAT PANEL (Make 3)

With Blue and straight needles, cast on 24 sts.

Row 1: Purl across.

Row 2 (Right side): Knit across.

Rows 3-7: Repeat Rows 1 and 2 twice, then repeat Row 1 once **more**.

Row 8: K7, P 10, K7.

Row 9: P6, K 12, P6.

Row 10: K5, P 14, K5.

Row 11: Purl across.

Row 12: Knit across.

Row 13: P4, K6, P1, K9, P4.

Row 14: K5, P8, K1, P6, K4.

Row 15: P4, K6, P1, K8, P5.

Row 16: K6, P7, K1, P5, K5.

Row 17: P5, K5, P1, K6, P7.

Row 18: K7, P6, K1, P4, K6.

Row 19: P6, K4, P1, K5, P8.

Row 20: K9, P4, K1, P3, K7.

Row 21: P7, K3, P1, K4, P9.

Row 22: K 10, P3, K1, P2, K8.

Row 23: P8, K2, P1, K2, P 11.

Row 24: K 11, P2, K1, P1, K9.

Row 25: P 11, K1, P 12.

Row 26: Knit across.

Row 27: Purl across.

Rows 28-37: Repeat Rows 26 and 27, 5 times.

Rows 38-151: Repeat Rows 8-37, 3 times; then repeat Rows 8-31 once **more**.

Slip stitches onto stitch holder.

ASSEMBLY

Using photo as a guide for placement and alternating Panels, whipstitch Panels together **(Fig. 10, page 46)**.

Odd how these things went, Carol mused. A group of mismatched personalities, four women with nothing in common, had come together and over the course of a few months, they'd become real friends.

TOP BORDER

Lydia's Tip: When stitches are picked up and knit one at a time, it prevents a ridge from forming on the wrong side, as it would if the stitches are only picked up and not knit until the next row.

The Border is worked separately across each side of the Blanket, using a yarn over to increase stitches and form a pattern. The Border is then sewn together at the corners.

With **right** side facing, slip sts from st holders onto circular needle: 96 sts.

Row 1: With Blue, knit across.

Row 2: Purl across.

Row 3: K1, YO *(Fig. 1a, page 43)*, knit across to last st, YO, K1.

Row 4: Knit across.

Rows 5-7: Repeat Rows 3 and 4 once, then repeat Row 3 once **more**.

Rows 8-18: Repeat Rows 2-7 once, then repeat Rows 2-6 once **more**.

Bind off all sts in **knit**.

BOTTOM BORDER

To pick up and knit stitches, pick up a stitch *(Figs. 9a & b, page 45)* and place it on the left needle, then knit the stitch.

With **right** side facing, using circular needle and Blue, pick up and knit 24 sts across each Boat Panel and 12 sts across each Cable Panel across bottom edge: 96 sts.

Work same as Top Border Rows 2-18.

SIDE BORDER (Make 2)

With **right** side facing, using circular needle and Blue, pick up and knit evenly across long edge.

Work same as Top Border Rows 2-18.

Sew corners together.

Weave in all yarn ends.

Design by Donita Dubil.

donovan diamonds

*Carol made this lilac blanket for Jacqueline's grandbaby.
The yarn is a wonderfully soft cotton terry. And Carol thinks
that the diamond pattern is simply a natural choice for
any baby whose last name is "Donovan."*

■■■□ **INTERMEDIATE**

Lydia's Tip: Using decreases that slant in opposite directions in combination with a yarn over is an effective way to form a pattern such as diamonds.

Finished Size: 35" x 48" (89 cm x 122 cm)

MATERIALS

Medium/Worsted Weight Yarn:
[3 ounces, 200 yards, 85 grams, 183 meters per skein]: 5 skeins
29" (73.5 cm) or 36" (91.5 cm) Circular knitting needle, size 8 (5 mm) **or** size needed for gauge
Yarn needle

GAUGE: In pattern, 20 sts = 6" (15.25 cm)

Gauge Swatch: 7¹/₂"w x 4"h (19 cm x 10 cm)
Cast on 27 sts.
Work same as Blanket for 23 rows.
Bind off all sts in knit.

BLANKET
Cast on 117 sts.

Rows 1-5: Knit across.

Row 6 (Right side)**:** K7, K2 tog *(Fig. 3, page 44)*, YO *(Fig. 1a, page 43)*, K8, ★ K2 tog, YO, K8; repeat from ★ across.

Row 7 AND ALL WRONG SIDE ROWS: K3, purl across to last 3 sts, K3.

When instructed to slip a stitch that will be used in a decrease, always slip as if to **knit**.

Row 8: K6, K2 tog, YO, K1, YO, [slip 1, K1, PSSO *(Figs. 5a & b, page 44)*], ★ K5, K2 tog, YO, K1, YO, slip 1, K1, PSSO; repeat from ★ across to last 6 sts, K6.

Instructions continued on page 29.

Carol wasn't sure what Jacqueline was working on these days. She'd started knitting scarves using an ultra-expensive yarn and then moved on to felting hats and purses. It was hard to keep up with Jacqueline's current projects because she leaped from one to another and seemed to have several in progress at a time.

a lesson on color

Now that Jacqueline is going on cruises all over the world, she's finding inspiration for new color combinations. She says the pattern for this light-weight baby blanket is easy, and the ripples remind her of sunsets on the Mediterranean.

■■■□ INTERMEDIATE

Lydia's Tip: Using the same decrease for each row causes the yarn over pattern to slant in the same direction as the decrease. The SSK slants to the left and the K2 together slants to the right. Alternating blocks made of opposite decreases will form a natural ripple on all of the edges. A crocheted edging is added for extra emphasis.

Finished Size: 33" (84 cm) square

MATERIALS

Fine/Sport Weight Yarn:
[2.5 ounces, 168 yards, 70 grams, 154 meters per skein]:
Purple – 2 skeins
Lime – 2 skeins
Turquoise – 2 skeins
Coral – 2 skeins
29" (73.5 cm) or 36" (91.5 cm) Circular knitting needle, size 4 (3.5 mm) **or** size needed for gauge
Crochet hook for Edging, size E (3.5 mm)
Tapestry needle

GAUGE: In pattern,
2 repeats (32 sts) = 5¼" (13.25 cm);
36 rows = 4" (10 cm)

Gauge Swatch: 6"w x 4"h (15.25 cm x 10 cm)
With Purple, cast on 37 sts.
Work same as Blanket for 36 rows.
Bind off all sts in knit.

BLANKET
With Purple, cast on 197 sts.

Rows 1 and 2: Knit across.

Row 3 (Right side): K2, (SSK, YO) 4 times *(Figs. 4a-c, page 44 and Fig. 1a, page 43)*, ★ K8, (SSK, YO) 4 times; repeat from ★ across to last 11 sts, K 11.

Row 4: Purl across.

Rows 5-10: Repeat Rows 3 and 4, 3 times.

Row 11: K 11, (YO, K2 tog) 4 times *(Fig. 3, page 44)*, ★ K8, (YO, K2 tog) 4 times; repeat from ★ across to last 2 sts, K2.

Row 12: Purl across.

Rows 13-18: Repeat Rows 11 and 12, 3 times.

Rows 19-34: Repeat Rows 3-18.

Rows 35 and 36: Knit across.

Repeat Rows 1-36 for pattern working 36 rows with each color in the following color sequence: Lime, Turquoise, Coral, Purple, Lime, Turquoise, Coral.

Bind off all sts in knit.

Instructions continued on page 28.

BORDER

Rnd 1: With **right** side facing, join Purple with sc in any corner *(see Crochet Stitches, page 47)*; sc evenly around entire blanket working 2 sc in each peak, skipping one st at each dip, and working 3 sc in each corner; join with slip st to first sc, finish off.

Rnds 2-4: Repeat Rnd 1 working in the following color sequence: Lime, Turquoise, Coral.

Weave in all yarn ends.

Design by Deborah Robson.

Jacqueline had discovered that so much of knitting was about choosing the textures and colors, which was something she hadn't considered before. She walked out of the class with the realization that she'd learned far more than the basic knitting stitches.

Donovan Diamonds continued from page 24.

Row 10: K5, K2 tog, YO, K3, YO, slip 1, K1, PSSO, ★ K3, K2 tog, YO, K3, YO, slip 1, K1, PSSO; repeat from ★ across to last 5 sts, K5.

Row 12: K4, K2 tog, YO, K1, YO, [slip 1, K2 tog, PSSO *(Fig. 7, page 45)*], YO, K1, YO, slip 1, K1, PSSO, ★ K1, K2 tog, YO, K1, YO, slip 1, K2 tog, PSSO, YO, K1, YO, slip 1, K1, PSSO; repeat from ★ across to last 4 sts, K4.

Row 14: K3, K2 tog, YO, K7, ★ YO, slip 1, K2 tog, PSSO, YO, K7; repeat from ★ across to last 5 sts, YO, slip 1, K1, PSSO, K3.

Row 16: K5, YO, slip 1, K2 tog, PSSO, YO, K1, YO, slip 1, K2 tog, PSSO, ★ YO, K3, YO, slip 1, K2 tog, PSSO, YO, K1, YO, slip 1, K2 tog, PSSO; repeat from ★ across to last 5 sts, YO, K5.

Row 18: K5, K2 tog, YO, K3, YO, slip 1, K1, PSSO, ★ K3, K2 tog, YO, K3, YO, slip 1, K1, PSSO; repeat from ★ across to last 5 sts, K5.

Row 20: K7, ★ YO, slip 1, K2 tog, PSSO, YO, K7; repeat from ★ across.

Repeat Rows 6-21 for pattern until Blanket measures approximately 47" (119.5 cm) from cast on edge, ending by working **Row 7.**

Last 5 Rows: Knit across.

Bind off all sts in **knit.**

Weave in all yarn ends.

Design by Carole Prior.

a day *in the* park

Apple-green yarn with a bright, wiggly cord running through it — Carol laughed when she saw it, then promptly bought enough for this baby blanket. The light-weight afghan is perfect for tucking into a stroller before a walk in the park.

 EASY

Lydia's Tip: A slightly different technique is used to form extra texture. The double yarn over is dropped off the needle on the following row, forming long enough stitches to cross over each other.

Finished Size: 36" x 42" (91.5 cm x 106.5 cm)

MATERIALS
Light/DK Weight Yarn:
[3.5 ounces, 250 yards, 100 grams, 230 meters per skein]: 6 skeins
29" (73.5 cm) or 36" (91.5 cm) Circular knitting needle, size 7 (4.5 mm) **or** size needed for gauge
Crochet hook (for fringe)
Yarn needle

GAUGE: In Stockinette Stitch, 18 sts = 4" (10 cm)

Gauge Swatch: 4" (10 cm) wide
Cast on 18 sts.
Rows 1-20: Work same as Blanket.
Bind off all sts.

BLANKET
Cast on 162 sts.

Row 1 (Right side)**:** Knit across.

Row 2: Purl across.

Row 3: K1, (YO twice, K1) across *(Fig. 1a, page 43)*: 484 sts.

Row 4: Slip 1 st as if to **purl**, (drop 2 YO's off needle, slip 1 st as if to purl) 5 times forming 6 long loops on the right needle, insert the left needle into the first 3 sts that were slipped on the right needle *(Fig. A)* and lift them over the last 3 slipped sts keeping them on the left needle, then slip the last 3 sts on the right needle onto the left needle *(Fig. B)*, purl each of the 6 sts, ★ with yarn forward, (drop 2 YO's off left needle, slip 1 st as if to purl) 6 times forming 6 long loops on the right needle, insert the left needle into the first 3 sts that were slipped on the right needle and lift them over the last 3 slipped sts keeping them on the left needle, then slip the last 3 sts on the right needle onto the left needle, purl each of the 6 sts; repeat from ★ across: 162 sts.

Fig. A   **Fig. B**

Rows 5-8: Repeat Rows 1 and 2 twice.

Repeat Rows 3-8 for pattern until Blanket measures approximately 42" (106.5 cm) from cast on edge, ending by working **Row 6**.

Bind off all sts in knit.

Weave in all yarn ends.

Holding 6 strands of yarn together and using photo as a guide for placement, add fringe at corners and in center of each pattern across short edges of Blanket *(Figs. 11a & b, page 46)*.

Design by Robin Villiers-Furze.

Cameron gazed up from the carpet where he sat sorting through his daddy's sock drawer. The nine-month-old grinned up at Carol guilelessly. "It's time for our walk," Carol told him. Cameron crawled rapidly toward the stroller. Once he reached it, he pulled himself into a standing position, then looked over his shoulder to be sure she'd noticed his feat. Cameron loved their walks.

alix's chocolate petits fours

Alix is almost as proud of this blanket as she is of her progress in cooking school. The colorful little rectangles remind her of the layers of cake and filling in petits fours, but she says this afghan is much easier to create than the dessert. That's because only one color is used for each row, and the "brickwork" effect is achieved by slipping stitches.

■■□□ **EASY**

Lydia's Tip: After a stitch is slipped, knit the next stitch with even tension to prevent puckering. The stitches should lie flat, side-by-side.

Finished Size: 30" (76 cm) square

MATERIALS

Medium/Worsted Weight Yarn: **4**
[4.5 ounces, 255 yards, 127 grams, 233 meters per skein]:
  Brown Variegated – 3 skeins
  Contrasting Variegated – 2 skeins
29" (73.5 cm) or 36" (91.5 cm) Circular knitting needle, size 8 (5 mm) **or** size needed for gauge
Markers
Yarn needle

GAUGE: In pattern,
  24 sts = 5" (12.75 cm);
  36 rows = 4" (10 cm)

Gauge Swatch: 4³/₄"w x 4¹/₄"h
(12 cm x 10.75 cm)

With Brown Variegated, cast on 23 sts.
Rows 1 and 2: Knit across.
Note: When instructed to slip a stitch, always slip as if to **purl** with yarn held to **wrong** side.
Row 3 (Right side)**:** With Contrasting Variegated, K1, slip 1, (K3, slip 1) across to last st, K1.
Row 4: K1, slip 1, (P3, slip 1) across to last st, K1.
Rows 5 and 6: With Brown Variegated, knit across.
Row 7: With Contrasting Variegated, (K1, slip 1) twice, (K3, slip 1) across to last 3 sts, K1, slip 1, K1.
Row 8: K1, slip 1, P1, slip 1, (P3, slip 1) across to last 3 sts, P1, slip 1, K1.
Rows 9 and 10: With Brown Variegated, knit across.
Rows 11-38: Repeat Rows 3-10, 3 times, then repeat Rows 3-6 once **more**.
Bind off all sts in knit.

Instructions continued on page 37.

Everyone had problems, Alix now realized, even if they lived in gorgeous apartments with million-dollar views. Over lunch she and Carol covered a lot of subjects, and after a while, it felt just as if they were in the knitting group at Lydia's shop. Alix had never expected to become friends with these women, but that was exactly what had happened. Even with Jacqueline.

lydia's lacy blocks

Fuzzy, bulky-weight yarn makes this little wrap as soft as a baby chick. The easy design creates blocks of lace, and the whole thing finishes quickly. Alix is planning on knitting a couple of these blankets to put away. She says it's always a good idea to look ahead to the future.

⬤⬤⬤◻ **INTERMEDIATE**

Lydia's Tip: The checkered bottom border continues along both side edges. A different decrease is used on the two alternating lace rows. Each type of decrease slants in a different direction. Be careful to keep the yarn over on the needle, especially when making the SSK decrease.

Finished Size: 29" x 31" (73.5 cm x 78.5 cm)

MATERIALS

  Bulky Weight Yarn:
  [3 ounces, 135 yards, 85 grams, 123 meters per skein]: 5 skeins
  29" (73.5 cm) or 36" (91.5 cm) Circular knitting needle, size 10 (6 mm) **or** size needed for gauge
  Yarn needle

GAUGE: In Stockinette Stitch,
  18 sts = 5" (12.75 cm);
  24 rows = 4" (10 cm)

BOTTOM BORDER
Cast on 105 sts.

Row 1: K3, (P3, K3) across.

Row 2: P3, (K3, P3) across.

Row 3: K3, (P3, K3) across.

Rows 4 and 5: P3, (K3, P3) across.

Row 6: K3, (P3, K3) across.

Row 7: P3, (K3, P3) across.

Row 8: K3, (P3, K3) across.

BODY
Row 1: K3, P3, knit across to last 6 sts, P3, K3.

Row 2: P3, K3, purl across to last 6 sts, K3, P3.

Rows 3 and 4: Repeat Rows 1 and 2.

Row 5: P3, knit across to last 3 sts, P3.

Row 6: K3, purl across to last 3 sts, K3.

Rows 7 and 8: Repeat Rows 5 and 6.

Instructions continued on page 36.

This has certainly been an eventful year. My original three class members are still with me and we share a deep bond. We're friends. Our Friday afternoon sessions are an ongoing social event — with knitting.

— Lydia

Row 9: K3, P3, K7, (YO, K2 tog) 4 times *(Figs. 1a, page 43 and Fig. 3, page 44)*, ★ K 10, (YO, K2 tog) 4 times; repeat from ★ across to last 12 sts, K6, P3, K3.

Row 10: P3, K3, purl across to last 6 sts, K3, P3.

Row 11: K3, P3, K6, (SSK, YO) 4 times *(Figs. 4a-c, page 44)*, ★ K 10 (SSK, YO) 4 times; repeat from ★ across to last 13 sts, K7, P3, K3.

Row 12: P3, K3, purl across to last 6 sts, K3, P3.

Row 13: P3, ★ K 10, (YO, K2 tog) 4 times; repeat from ★ across to last 12 sts, K9, P3.

Row 14: K3, purl across to last 3 sts, K3.

Row 15: P3, K9, (SSK, YO) 4 times, K 10, ★ (SSK, YO) 4 times, K 10; repeat from ★ across to last 3 sts, P3.

Row 16: K3, purl across to last 3 sts, K3.

Rows 17-20: Repeat Rows 9-12.

Row 21: P3, K 19, (YO, K2 tog) 4 times, ★ K 10, (YO, K2 tog) 4 times; repeat from ★ across to last 21 sts, K 18, P3.

Row 22: K3, purl across to last 3 sts, K3.

Row 23: P3, K 18, (SSK, YO) 4 times, ★ K 10, (SSK, YO) 4 times; repeat from ★ across to last 22 sts, K 19, P3.

Row 24: K3, purl across to last 3 sts, K3.

Row 25: K3, P3, K 16, (YO, K2 tog) 4 times, ★ K 10, (YO, K2 tog) 4 times; repeat from ★ across to last 21 sts, K 15, P3, K3.

Row 26: P3, K3, purl across to last 6 sts, K3, P3.

Row 27: K3, P3, K 15, (SSK, YO) 4 times, ★ K 10, (SSK, YO) 4 times; repeat from ★ across to last 22 sts, K 16, P3, K3.

Rows 28-32: Repeat Rows 20-24.

Repeat Rows 9-32 for pattern until Blanket measures approximately 28½" (72.5 cm) from cast on edge, ending by working **Row 20**.

Next 4 Rows: Repeat Rows 5 and 6 of Body twice.

Next 4 Rows: Repeat Rows 1 and 2 of Body twice.

TOP BORDER
Row 1: P3, (K3, P3) across.

Row 2: K3, (P3, K3) across.

Row 3: P3, (K3, P3) across.

Rows 4 and 5: K3, (P3, K3) across.

Row 6: P3, (K3, P3) across.

Row 7: K3, (P3, K3) across.

Row 8: P3, (K3, P3) across.

Bind off all sts in pattern.

Weave in all yarn ends.

Design by Deborah Robson.

Alix's Chocolate Petits Fours continued from page 32.

BLANKET

With Brown Variegated, cast on 145 sts.

Rows 1-21: Knit across.

Row 22: K 10, place marker *(see Markers, page 44)*, knit across to last 10 sts, place marker, knit across, drop yarn.

When instructed to slip a stitch, always slip as if to **purl** with yarn held to **wrong** side.

Row 23 (Right side): With Contrasting Variegated, knit across to first marker, slip 1, (K3, slip 1) across to next marker, knit across.

Row 24: Knit across to first marker, slip 1, (P3, slip 1) across to next marker, knit across.

Rows 25 and 26: With Brown Variegated, knit across.

Row 27: With Contrasting Variegated, knit across to first marker, slip 1, K1, slip 1, (K3, slip 1) across to within 2 sts of next marker, K1, slip 1, knit across.

Row 28: Knit across to first marker, slip 1, P1, slip 1, (P3, slip 1) across to within 2 sts of next marker, P1, slip 1, knit across.

Rows 29 and 30: With Brown Variegated, knit across.

Repeat Rows 23-30 for pattern until Blanket measures approximately 27¾" (70.5 cm) from cast on edge, ending by working **Row 24.**

Last 22 rows: With Brown Variegated, knit across.

Bind off all sts in knit.

Weave in all yarn ends.

Design by Deborah Robson.

thank you for helping
warm up
america!

Warm Up America! was started in 1991 by a Wisconsin yarn retailer named Evie Rosen. Evie decided to help the homeless by asking her customers, friends, and community to knit or crochet 7" x 9" blocks that would be joined into afghans. The efforts of those original contributors spread across the nation. To date, more than 80,000 afghans have been donated to battered women's shelters, victims of natural disaster, the homeless, and many others who are in need.

With your purchase of this *Knit Along with Debbie Macomber* pattern book, you have already helped the Warm Up America! Foundation. Debbie is generously donating all her profits from the sale of this pattern book to Warm Up America! And Leisure Arts, Inc. is also donating a portion of its proceeds.

But there is still so much more **you** can do to help, and with so little effort. Debbie urges everyone who uses the patterns in this book to take a few minutes to knit a 7" x 9" block for this worthy cause. To help you get started, she's providing these three block patterns. Please take time to create a block for Warm Up America!, and ask your friends to get involved, as well.

If you are able to provide a completed afghan, Warm Up America! requests that you donate it directly to your local chapter of the American Red Cross or to any charity or social services agency in your community. If you require assistance in assembling the blocks into an afghan, please include your name and address inside the packaging and ship your 7" x 9" blocks to:

Warm Up America! Foundation
2500 Lowell Road
Ranlo, NC 28054

Remember, just a little bit of yarn can make big difference to someone in need!

Basic patchwork afghans are made of forty-nine 7" x 9" (18 cm x 23 cm) rectangular Blocks that are sewn together. Any pattern stitch can be used for the rectangle, including the three following Blocks. Use acrylic medium/worsted weight yarn and size 8 (5 mm) straight knitting needles or size needed to obtain the gauge of 9 stitches to 2" (5 cm).

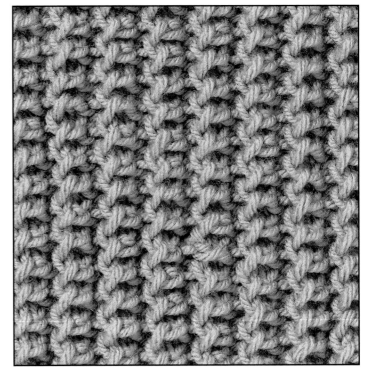

SEED STITCH BLOCK
Multiple of 2 sts.

Cast on 32 sts.

Row 1 (Right side)**:** (K1, P1) across.

Row 2: (P1, K1) across.

Repeat Rows 1 and 2 for pattern until Block measures approximately 9" (23 cm) from cast on edge.

Bind off all sts in pattern.

CLUSTER RIB BLOCK
Multiple of 3 sts + 1.

Cast on 34 sts.

Row 1 (Right side)**:** P1, (K2, P1) across.

Row 2: K1, ★ YO *(Fig. 1a, page 43)*, K2, with left needle bring the YO over the 2 knit sts and off the right needle, K1; repeat from ★ across.

Repeat Rows 1 and 2 for pattern until Block measures approximately 9" (23 cm) from cast on edge, ending by working **Row 2**.

Bind off all sts in pattern.

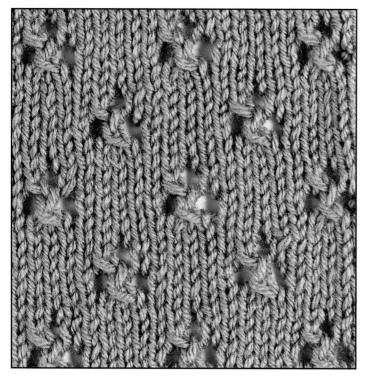

CLOVERLEAF EYELET BLOCK
Multiple of 8 sts + 7.

When instructed to slip a stitch that will be used in a decrease, always slip as if to **knit**.

Cast on 31 sts.

Row 1 AND ALL WRONG SIDE ROWS: Purl across.

Row 2: Knit across.

Row 4: K2, YO (*Fig. 1a, page 43*), [slip 1, K2 tog, PSSO (*Fig. 7, page 45*)], ★ YO, K5, YO, slip 1, K2 tog, PSSO; repeat from ★ across to last 2 sts, YO, K2.

Row 6: K3, YO, SSK (*Figs. 4a-c, page 44*), (K6, YO, SSK) across to last 2 sts, K2.

Row 8: Knit across.

Row 10: K6, YO, slip 1, K2 tog, PSSO, ★ YO, K5, YO, slip 1, K2 tog, PSSO; repeat from ★ across to last 6 sts, YO, K6.

Row 12: K7, (YO, SSK, K6) across.

Repeat Rows 1-12 for pattern until Block measures approximately 9" (23 cm) from cast on edge, ending by working **Row 3 or 9.**

Bind off all sts in knit.

ASSEMBLY
Whipstitch Blocks together (*Fig. 10, page 46*), forming 7 vertical strips of 7 Blocks each and measuring 7" x 63" (18 cm x 160 cm); whipstitch strips together in same manner.

Weave in all yarn ends.

general instructions

ABBREVIATIONS

cm	centimeters
K	knit
mm	millimeters
P	purl
PSSO	pass slipped stitch(es) over
Rnd(s)	round(s)
RT	Right Twist
sc	single crochet(s)
SSK	slip, slip, knit
st(s)	stitch(es)
tog	together
YO	yarn over

★ — work instructions following ★ as many **more** times as indicated in addition to the first time.

( ) or [ ] — work enclosed instructions **as many** times as specified by the number immediately following **or** work all enclosed instructions in the stitch or space indicated **or** contains explanatory remarks.

GAUGE

Exact gauge is **essential** for proper size. Before beginning your Blanket, make a sample swatch in the yarn and needle specified as given in the individual instructions or in Stockinette Stitch. After completing the swatch, measure it, counting your stitches and rows carefully. If your swatch is larger or smaller than specified, **make another, changing needle size to get the correct gauge**. Keep trying until you find the size needles that will give you the specified gauge. Once proper gauge is obtained, measure width of Blanket approximately every 3" (7.5 cm) to be sure gauge remains consistent.

KNIT & CROCHET TERMINOLOGY		
UNITED STATES		**INTERNATIONAL**
gauge	=	tension
bind off	=	cast off
yarn over (YO)	=	yarn forward (yfwd) **or**
		yarn around needle (yrn)
slip stitch (slip st)	=	single crochet (sc)
single crochet (sc)	=	double crochet (dc)

MARKERS

As a convenience to you, we have used markers to help distinguish the beginning of a pattern. Place markers as instructed. You may use purchased markers or tie a length of contrasting color yarn around the needle. When you reach a marker on each row, slip it from the left needle to the right needle; remove it when no longer needed.

YARN WEIGHTS

Yarn Weight Symbol & Names	SUPER FINE 1	FINE 2	LIGHT 3	MEDIUM 4	BULKY 5	SUPER BULKY 6
Type of Yarns in Category	Sock, Fingering Baby	Sport, Baby	DK, Light Worsted	Worsted, Afghan, Aran	Chunky, Craft, Rug	Bulky, Roving

SKILL LEVELS

■□□□ BEGINNER	Projects for first-time knitters using basic knit and purl stitches. Minimal shaping.
■■□□ EASY	Projects using basic stitches, repetitive stitch patterns, simple color changes, and simple shaping and finishing.
■■■□ INTERMEDIATE	Projects with a variety of stitches, such as basic cables and lace, simple intarsia, double-pointed needles and knitting in the round needle techniques, mid-level shaping and finishing.
■■■■ EXPERIENCED	Projects using advanced techniques and stitches, such as short rows, fair isle, more intricate intarsia, cables, lace patterns, and numerous color changes.

KNITTING NEEDLES

U.S.	0	1	2	3	4	5	6	7	8	9	10	10½	11	13	15	17
U.K.	13	12	11	10	9	8	7	6	5	4	3	2	1	00	000	---
Metric - mm	2	2.25	2.75	3.25	3.5	3.75	4	4.5	5	5.5	6	6.5	8	9	10	12.75

ALUMINUM CROCHET HOOKS

U.S.	B-1	C-2	D-3	E-4	F-5	G-6	H-8	I-9	J-10	K-10½	N	P	Q
Metric - mm	2.25	2.75	3.25	3.5	3.75	4	5	5.5	6	6.5	9	10	15

YARN OVERS

A Yarn over *(abbreviated YO)* is simply placing the yarn over the right needle creating an extra stitch. Since the Yarn Over does produce a hole in the knit fabric, it is used for a lacy effect. On the row following a Yarn Over, you must be careful to keep it on the needle and treat it as a stitch by knitting or purling it as instructed.

To make a yarn over, you'll loop the yarn over the needle like you would to knit or purl a stitch, bringing it either to the front or the back of the piece so that it'll be ready to work the next stitch, creating a new stitch on the needle as follows:

After a knit stitch, before a knit stitch
Bring the yarn forward **between** the needles, then back **over** the top of the right hand needle, so that it is now in position to knit the next stitch *(Fig. 1a)*.

Fig. 1a

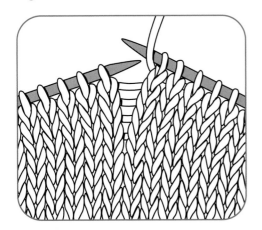

After a purl stitch, before a knit stitch
Take the yarn **over** the right hand needle to the back, so that it is now in position to knit the next stitch *(Fig. 1b)*.

Fig. 1b

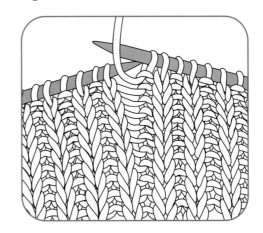

After a knit stitch, before a purl stitch
Bring the yarn forward **between** the needles, then back **over** the top of the right hand needle and forward **between** the needles again, so that it is now in position to purl the next stitch *(Fig. 1c)*.

Fig. 1c

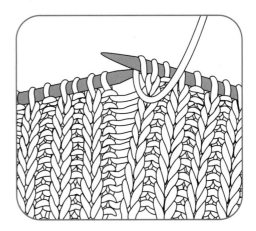

KNIT INCREASE

Knit the next stitch but do **not** slip the old stitch off the left needle **(Fig. 2a)**. Insert the right needle into the **back** loop of the **same** stitch and knit it **(Fig. 2b)**, then slip the old stitch off the left needle.

Fig. 2a

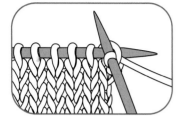

Fig. 2b

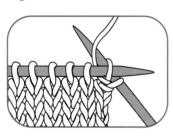

KNIT 2 TOGETHER
(abbreviated K2 tog)

Insert the right needle into the **front** of the first two stitches on the left needle as if to **knit (Fig. 3)**, then **knit** them together as if they were one stitch.

Fig. 3

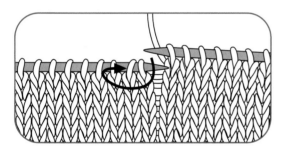

SLIP, SLIP, KNIT
(abbreviated SSK)

With yarn in back of work, separately slip two stitches as if to **knit (Fig. 4a)**. Insert the **left** needle into the **front** of both slipped stitches **(Fig. 4b)** and knit them together as if they were one stitch **(Fig. 4c)**.

Fig. 4a   **Fig. 4b**

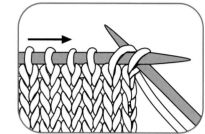

Fig. 4c

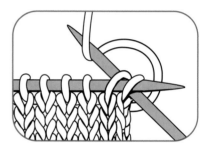

SLIP 1, KNIT 1, PASS SLIPPED STITCH OVER
(abbreviated slip 1, K1, PSSO)

Slip one stitch as if to **knit (Fig. 5a)**. Knit the next stitch. With the left needle, bring the slipped stitch over the knit stitch **(Fig. 5b)** and off the needle.

Fig. 5a

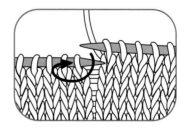

Fig. 5b

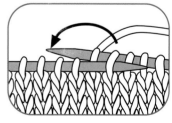

SLIP 1, KNIT 2, PASS SLIPPED STITCH OVER
(abbreviated slip 1, K2, PSSO)

Slip one stitch as if to **knit** *(Fig. 5a, page 44)*. Knit the next two stitches. With the left needle, bring the slipped stitch over the two knit stitches *(Fig. 6)* and off the needle.

Fig. 6

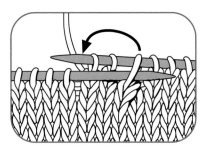

SLIP 1, KNIT 2 TOGETHER, PASS SLIPPED STITCH OVER
(abbreviated slip 1, K2 tog, PSSO)

Slip one stitch as if to **knit** *(Fig. 5a, page 44)*, then knit the next two stitches together *(Fig. 3, page 44)*. With the left needle, bring the slipped stitch over the stitch just made *(Fig. 7)* and off the needle.

Fig. 7

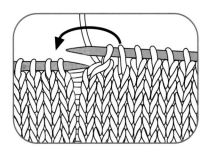

PURL 2 TOGETHER
(abbreviated P2 tog)

Insert the right needle into the **front** of the first two stitches on the left needle as if to **purl** *(Fig. 8)*, then **purl** them together as if they were one stitch.

Fig. 8

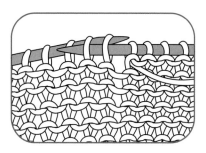

PICKING UP STITCHES

When instructed to pick up stitches, insert the needle from the **front** to the **back** under two strands at the edge of the worked piece *(Figs. 9 a & b)*. Put the yarn around the needle as if to **knit**, then bring the needle with the yarn back through the stitch to the right side, resulting in a stitch on the needle.

Repeat this along the edge, picking up the required number of stitches.

A crochet hook may be helpful to pull yarn through.

Fig. 9a   **Fig. 9b**

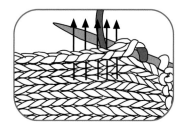 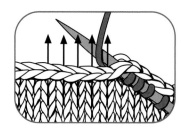

WHIPSTITCH

With **right** sides together, sew through both pieces once to secure the beginning of the seam, leaving an ample yarn end to weave in later. Insert the needle from **front** to **back** through one strand on each piece *(Fig. 10)*. Bring the needle around and insert it from **front** to **back** through the next strand on both pieces.

Repeat along the edge.

Fig. 10

FRINGE

Cut a piece of cardboard 7" (18 cm) square. Wind the yarn **loosely** and **evenly** around the cardboard until the card is filled, then cut across one end; repeat as needed.

Hold together as many strands as specified in individual instructions; fold in half. With **wrong** side facing and using a crochet hook, draw the folded end up through a stitch and pull the loose ends through the folded end *(Fig. 11a)*; draw the knot up **tightly** *(Fig. 11b)*. Repeat, spacing as specified in individual instructions. Lay Blanket flat on a hard surface and trim the ends.

Fig. 11a **Fig. 11b**

BASIC CROCHET STITCHES

YARN OVER *(abbreviated YO)*
Bring the yarn over the top of the hook from back to front, catching the yarn with the hook and turning the hook slightly toward you to keep the yarn from slipping off *(Fig. 12)*.

Fig. 12
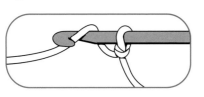

SINGLE CROCHET *(abbreviated sc)*
Insert hook in stitch indicated, YO and pull up a loop, YO and draw through both loops on hook *(Fig. 13)*.

Fig. 13

JOINING WITH SC
Begin with a slip knot on the hook. Insert hook in stitch indicated, YO and pull up a loop, YO and draw through both loops on hook *(Fig. 14)*.

Fig. 14
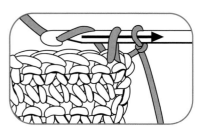

SLIP STITCH *(abbreviated slip st)*
Insert hook in stitch indicated, YO and draw through st and through loop on hook *(Fig. 15)*.

Fig. 15

yarn information

The blankets in this leaflet were made using a variety of yarns. Any brand of yarn in the specified weight may be used. It is best to refer to the yardage/meters when determining how many balls or skeins to purchase. Remember, to arrive at the finished size, it is the GAUGE/TENSION that is important, not the brand of yarn.

For your convenience, listed below are the specific yarns used to create our photography models.

BABY BLOCKS
Bernat® Satin
#04420 Sea Shell

CAROL'S SUNSHINE
Bernat® Cottontots™
#90615 Sunshine

SLEEPY IN SEATTLE
Bernat® Baby Boucle´
#36923 Flower Power

ONLY THE FINEST FOR AMELIA
Caron® Simply Soft Baby Sport
#2501 White

LYDIA'S BABY CABLES
Caron® Simply Soft
#9701 White

BOATS FOR CAMERON
Lion Brand® Chunky USA
White - #100 Snowcap White
Blue - #106 Pacific Blue

DONOVAN DIAMONDS
Red Heart®Baby Teri™
#9145 Lilac

A LESSON ON COLOR
Lion Brand® Micro Spun
Purple - #147 Purple
Green - #194 Lime
Turquoise - #148 Turquoise
Coral - #103 Coral

A DAY IN THE PARK
TLC® Wiggles™
#0727 Green

ALIX'S CHOCOLATE PETITS FOURS
TLC® Essential™
Brown Variegated - #2953 Brownberry
Contrasting Variegated - #2943 High Plains

LYDIA'S LACY BLOCKS
Lion Brand® Jiffy®
#157 Pastel Yellow

SEED STITCH BLOCK
Red Heart® Super Saver®
#0332 Ranch Red

CLUSTER RIB BLOCK
Caron® Perfect Match®
#7708 Slate Blue

CLOVERLEAF EYELET BLOCK
Red Heart® Super Saver®
#631 Light Sage